Two Nights to Remember

Carl Anderson & Alfred Steber

Illustrated by Frederic R. Aber
Cover design by Bob Peterson

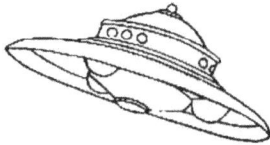

SAUCERIAN PUBLISHER
Original Sources in Ufology

ISBN: **978-1-955087-66-7**

9 781955 087667

© 2024, Saucerian Publisher

INTRODUCTION

Carl Anderson had his first encounter with a flying object on April 3, 1954. It happened near the small town of Desert Center, California, where, among other things, G. Adamsky's famous encounter with extraterrestrial beings took place. It is said that he did not get to this place in the desert by accident, because everything was actually the result of some persistent mysterious voice that Anderson heard in his head before this meeting. At night, together with his wife and daughter, he saw a strange object hovering just above the ground, which was about 20 meters in diameter. They could not move during the observation of the object.

When Anderson told others about his story, he learned that another family who was camping nearby at the same time had experienced the same story. From that moment on, in the months that followed, Anderson experienced several more similar incidents. The effect of the contacts was the activation of his alleged media abilities.

Thanks to them, on February 25, 1957, he receives a kind of message, or rather a message. The content was a prediction of the near future. There were supposed to be local natural disasters, accompanied by a change in the movement of the earth's axis and the location of the poles, which would be a tool for the spiritual purification of Mother Earth. At the same time, about one third of the population perishes. However, just before that cataclysmic series, a large number of human individuals will be saved by teleportation into spaceships.

In other messages that Anderson received, there is also a kind of general reference to the fact that there are some spatial zones on our planet in which people will be able to find relative safety in times of disasters.

About a year after these series of mental communications, Anderson's first physical contact with extraterrestrial beings occurred. This event was supposed to happen on June 27, 1958. However, not in the desert or some remote place, as is often the case, but right in the house where the contactee lived. When he was returning from his regular walk, a man who claimed to be from Mars appeared out of nowhere. The "alien" said that many extraterrestrial individuals currently living in incarnated human bodies come from Mars. The aliens are said to have tried several times to contact the governments of several Earth powers, but with negative results. Therefore, they prefer to try to establish contact with selected simple individuals, to whom they convey various messages in a mental form. Before disappearing again in an equally mysterious manner, he told Anderson that he would receive another very important message within a week.

What was the subject of the following message is not known exactly. However, emphasis was also placed on the negative impact of atomic energy.

During one of his last encounters with aliens, Anderson was handed a strange jasper about the size of a walnut that was said to have come from Mars. The unique frequency of this mineral allowed for special healing abilities, which Anderson demonstrated at the 1960 World Congress of Ufologists in Wiesbaden. The contacts are said to have continued.

Editor
Saucerian Publisher

Two Nights to Remember

I wish to express my sincere thanks to Mr. Frederic R. Aber of Garden Grove, California, for his painstaking efforts in drawing the wonderful sketches contained within this book. Mr. Aber was extremely well qualified to sketch the Spacecraft inasmuch as he has witnessed the very same type of craft at close range in the California deserts.

CARL A. ANDERSON

Two Nights to Remember

FOREWORD

After more than a decade of careful investigation of flying saucer sightings by the Air Force and other agencies of the government together with the tens of thousands of sightings by civilian observers all over the world, it might seem unnecessary to add any further sightings to the enormous number of wellauthenticated ones now on file. This would be true there the purpose merely to establish the existence of flying saucers, for their existence has now been thoroughly established beyond the shadow of a doubt by official sources.

The writings of Keyhoe, Ruppelt, Wilkins, Jessup, Michel and others have left little to be said in regard to mere sightings, and the release of Air Force data in the recent motion picture "Unidentified Flying Objects." has made the public thoroughly aware of the reality of what is commonly called "flying saucers" although the government agencies prefer to use the term "Unidentified Flying Objects." The reason for this preference is quite obviuus. as this very term is a clear confession that after more than ten years of intensive official Investigation they still do not know what they are.

Many people surmise that the Air Force possesses more information than it is willing to divulge and may have arrived at very definite ideas about the kind of UFO we call Flying Saucers. Obviously they do not consider them all to be harmless in the face of their continuing loss of planes and pilots in encounters with UFO. This accounts for application of security restrictions on some of the Air Force investigations and reports. This point of view has been developed in a recent publication entitled "Spacemen, Friends and Foes."

That there could be anything sinister connected with the Flying Saucers will be somewhat disconcerting to those who feel certain that they are coming here from other planets to help their human brothers on earth, perhaps as the forerunners of the return of Christ to earth. Certainly no one would want to deprive them of this reassurance. Consequently, anything that will throw further light upon the real nature of the Flying Saucers and their purpose in visiting us is of tremendous importance. It is for this reason that we have decided to present for your consideration the experience of Carl Anderson and family while spending the night in the desert.

Unlike most saucer sightings and contacts the experience of the Anderson family was witnessed by all of them and is supported by the sworn testimony of several other people. Usually the encounter with a Flying Saucer takes place when one is in a remote and isolated spot, and because there are no witnesses the observer is very reluctant to tell anyone about his experience lest he be thought to be either Iying or the victim of an hallucination. Consequently the public loses the opportunity to learn about many of the most spectacular of these happenings.

Two Nights to Remember

Were this merely another of these mysterious and and unknown events there would be little point in relating it for they have become a rather common occurrence, but there are a number of very strang. and significant factors involved in the Anderson experience which may throw considerable light upon the nature of the force field surrounding these ships and the nature and unusual powers and understanding of the occupants of the saucer who, in this case, were definitely friendly and sympathetic as shown by their maneuvers.

We believe you will find this very enlightening. It will also show that some of the saucer operators are friendly disposed, notwithstanding any doubts the Air Force may have as to flying saucers in general. Perhaps their encounters with them may justify their suspicion of the intention of the the operators of the flying saucers who may also be justified in regarding our ships as hostile, being as a rule heavily armed jet interceptors built and equipped to destroy alien craft.

There has been considerable evidence from all parts of the world that the peculiar color changes witnessed by Mr. Anderson and family have been a significant part of many well authenticated saucer sightings. l or example on December second of this year five mysterious lights were seen in the sky near San Luis Obispo when it was too light for stars. A United Press dispatch states that three police officers and a newspaper reporter watched the lights for forty-five minutes and described them as having a pulsating red glow, then changing to blue and finally to white.

There is undoubtedly some definite significance to this sequence of colors Is it part of a system of communication or does it have something to do with the frequency of their force field? Read Mr. Anderson's description of these changes and what followed and perhaps you may find a imitating segment of the jigsaw puzzle which will explain something of the purposes of the Flying: Saucers and by they do not land in our midst.

Certainly if the saucer occupants are able to do the things described in this book they are very desirable friends to have around. Let us hope we can learn more about their helpful activities and the devices by which they can bring about such startling effects.

Perhaps when we have learned more about the nature of the force field surrounding their ships and the danger involved in coming in too close a proximity to it, we will understand why they are reluctant to approach our regular landing fields, aside from the danger of being taken for enemy aircraft. Apparently they have more consideration for earthlings than has been accorded them. That the force field of flying saucers and spaceships could be dangerous has been somewhat recognized, but if such a field can produce some of the effects described by Mr. Anderson then the power is of a different type than has been supposed and able to produce vastly more far-reaching consequences. We should learn more about it.

The most remarkable experience of all during the two nights on the desert was the amazing instant healing of a painful injury through the mediation of the Space People. The method used is still a complete mystery, but it may also have something to do with the powerful radiations generated by the force field of the ship.

FRANKIN THOMAS

ABOUT THE AUTHOR

Carl A. Anderson was born on the 9th day of November in the year 1913, in the small seacoast town of Wellfleet, Massachusetts in Barnstable County, on Cape Cod.

He was christened George Everett Avery the son of the former Dorothy Rich of East Boston and George K. Avery of Londonderry, New Hampshire.

When young George was still an infant his mother and father separated. The father was seen no more. Young Dorothy Avery tried desperately to earn enough money to properly rear her son. But illness and misfortune intervened. and when the baby had reached the age of five, she tearfully turned him over to an adoption agency realizing that people of better financial stancling could give her son the education and upbringing that she never would be able to do.

Shortly after this young George was adopted by a lonely Swedish couple, Oscar O. Anderson and his wife Nellie. Young George's name was now legally changed to Carl Arthur Anderson. At first the Anclersons lived in the town of Arlington, Massachusetts. then later moved to the small town of South Levant Maine, where they bought a large farm. It was here that Carl grew up and lived very close to nature, taking great delight in roaming through the fields and forests and learning the habits of the wild life.

He used to sit for hours in the quiet stillness of the long summer evenings and gaze in wonderment at the myriad of stars in the cloudless heavens and marvel at God's handiwork, and wonder how many other far distant worlds were inhabited by people much the same as we. As he grew older, the more firm his convictions became that this was the case, and he felt that one day he would know the truth.

He graduated from high school in the town of Carmel, Maine, in the year 1930. Having worked as an electrician's helper for several years during summer vacations, Carl decided against becoming a farmer and in 1930 went to Massachusetts where he got a job in a large radio factory in Lawrence. Here he worked with the lovely girl who was to become his wife. They were married at Keene, New Hampshire on Jan. 30, 1932.

In 1939 he went to work as Maintenance Electrician for a large knitting mill in the town of Canton, Massachusetts. In 1941 Carl passed a Civil Service examination with flying colors and accepted a position with the U. S. Navy Dept. at Boston. In 1943 he was transferred to Long Beach, California, where he still works, and lives with his family.

TWO NIGHTS TO REMEMBER

I guess when it comes to Flying Saucers, or spacecraft from other worlds, that we are all rather dubious at first. Seeing is believing. I now believe.

It happened on Sunday, April 4th, 1954. Having been reared in the country and being very close to nature I like nothing better than to camp out under the stars in the mountains and in the deserts. Thus it was that my lovely wife. Stella, our youngest daughter, Betty Ann. our son, Bobby, and I, started on April 3rd. 1954, for a quiet and peaceful camping trip in the great Mojave desert of California.

The kids were elated at the thought of going camping Bobby and Betty helped arrange our nine by nine umbrella tent in the back of the family car, as well as the Coleman lantern. the three burner gasoline stove. folding, table. chairs. cots, air mattresses. and all of the other essentials for a perfect weekend.

During this time. needless to say. .Stella was busily engaged in makings sure that nothing was overlooked in the way of food. for as you know, when you are out in the middle of the desert, you just don't run down to the corner store and get a loaf of bread or a quart of milk. Also water, the most precious thing of all in the desert. must be taken in sufficient quantity, not only for making coffee but for drinking, cooking, washing dishes, something we try to avoid as much as possible

9

by using paper plates which can be burned.

But there is always the possibility of a radiator hose breaking or a water pump leaking, and an overheated motor on the desert is not the most pleasant thing to anticipate miles from civilization. After carefully checking our supplies and making sure we had plenty of warm blankets, sweaters, jackets, etc., for as you know it can get awfully cold on the desert before the sun comes up again to warm the sands, we at last decided we were ready to leave.

We all looked forward to a wonderful weekend, since it would not be too hot at this time of year and spring was in the air. Desert Cacti would also be in bloom.

As we were about to back our car from the driveway of our home, who should drive up but my brother-in-law, Jim, and his wife, Terry.

As Jim stepped from his car with his usual smile he called to Stella:

"Hi, Sis. Terry and I are going camping. How about joining us."
"Well now, that is a coincidence," I explained. "We were just leaving for the desert."

"So are we," replied Terry.

I called to Jim: "You back out and I'll lead the way."

"Where are we going?" asked Jim as he forced his way into his Dodge Coupe beside Terry. His front seat had been moved forward to make room for all of their

camping
gear.

"Let's go down near Desert Hot Springs," I replied.
"We have to wait for Harold," cried Terry. Harold is
my wife's other brother.

"Is he going too?" I called, as the cars started roll
down the drive.

"Oh, yes," shouted Jim. "He should be here any
minute. He stopped to gas up." Just then we heard
the familiar wolf whistle Harold had installed the
previous weekend, and
up rolled Harold and his wife, Eleanor.

"Where're we going?" grinned Harold as he slammed
the door of his 1946 Buick.

"Carl says he'll take US to Desert Hot Springs; we'll
follow," replied Jim.

After looking back to make sure everything was in
readiness, I started off in the lead, With Jim and
Terry behind me and Harold and Eleanor at the rear.
As we drove east on Highway 18, Stella and I talked of
many things. eve wondered if we would see any cactus
in bloom at this time of year., also the desert primrose
and other wild flowers that can be seen only in such
dry and barren spots. Now and then Betty or Bob
would comment or ask questions.

"I hope we see a flying saucer" exclaimed Bob. "They
say they have been landing in the desert."

Two Nights to Remember

"Yes," I replied. "I wonder if we will."

Suddenly, as if in answer to my question. a very strange feeling ran down mv spine. It was not like a cold chill, but more like a series of electrical shocks. This happened three times in success on. Somehow, I felt that I had established mental contact with someone outside of the boundries of this earth. I did not mention this to the others as I thought they would think I had suddenly gone mad. But I could not hide my feelings and my wife knew that something was on my mind.

She asked me several times why I was so quiet. I could not help thinking about the many reports that were being made of the numerous sightings of spacecraft and I wondered about the people who were in then. I reasoned that if these people were so far advanced in air travel, then they must also be many years ahead of Earthlings in all other ways. I seemed to picture them living in perfection, not knowing the terrors of warfare. Having no sickness, no need for hospitals, no doctors. no crime, therefore no penal institutions. using a system far different than our own monetary set-up. Thereby eliminating want and poverty. to say nothing of income taxes.

I could picture a land of milk and honey. Then the thought occurred to me that if such were the case - if there were no illness nor worry, nor heartache - how about their lifespan? Did they live perhaps one hundred years? Or maybe a thousand? Then I reasoned: Perhaps they never die. If such were the case. little wonder they did not make mass landings. Why should they risk being contaminated by us sickly, puny Earthlings who spend billions of dollars trying to develop new and more deadly weapons that perhaps eventually may wipe all trace of mankind from the face of this globe.

I wondered if God had not placed people on other worlds, as he did this one, in the beginning, and perhaps these people had lived according to the laws of the Creator and instead of retrogressing by sin, had progressed far beyond our imagination. Were these people the perfect {Creation even as our Saviour Christ? Were these people actually .- Angels?

Why not? Does not our Holy Bible refer to spacecraft and people who come out of space in times of great crisis to be of assistance? Was not Elijah taken to heaven in a fiery chariot? Could not the chariot have been a spacecraft? Where is heaven? Is it perhaps another world? Did not Christ say there are worlds without number? What is a wheel within a wheel? What is a flying roll? There are any number of Biblical references that could mean spacecraft or flying saucers.

And what of the people who ride in them? We know they must be far superior to us. Are they really Angels? Oh, no, Angels have wings! But do they? Are Angels part man and part bird? Or is this a myth - like the legendary, part woman and part fish, mermaid? Is it not entirely possible that Angels are really people like us that have lived according to the Creator's divine laws? who do not sin and have thus reached a state of perfection? Did the old writers of the dark dim past picture these supreme beings with wings like birds in order to convey the meaning of them being able to come from out of space, or fly anywhere they chose?

Is it not possible that we may be nearing another great catastrophe? such as in the time of the great flood? Will the rapidly increasing ice cap now building up at the South Pole at the rate of seven trillion tons a year, one day hurl the earth from its present orbit. Does it not say in Revelations that the earth will stagger like a drunken man, and whole continents will be changed? Does not the Bible say that even the Angels in Heaven do not know the day or the hour. Is it possible that they know it can't be long now, and are standing by with millions of spacecraft to save those who have lived with right intent toward God and their fellow men.

All of these things flashed through my mind as I drove steadily toward my destination. I wondered if all of these things could not be so. Yet I did not dare at that time to voice any opinions. Then I began to understand why many people were so reluctant to report saucer sightings. They would surely be branded as screwballs or crackpots. I, myself, am now in that category, having been put in that class by those individuals who refuse to expand the scope of their narrow-minded personal convictions. Sure, I could be wrong.

Likewise the skeptics also could be wrong. By this time? some of the readers who disagree with the foregoing conclusions no doubt are branding me as an atheist or one who disbelieves in out Holy Bible. I wish to make it very clear here and now that this very definitely is not the case. I believe one hundred percent in God our Holy Creator and in Christ our

Saviour, and in the word of God as set forth in our Holy Bible. But I also like to be broad-minded enough to realize that our Bible is the oldest Books we have, that it has been destroyed and rewritten many, many times in many different languages.

Also the ancients were exceptionally superstitious and the possibility of error is not to be overlooked. Also many passages in the Bible may have a symbolic orallegorical meaning. butte know for a very definite fact that thousands of predictions as set forth in our Bible have come true. We therefore have no reason to doubt its contents. Therefore the remaining prophecies will also come to pass. It does say that there shall be signs and wonders in the skies, that heavenly hosts shall come out of the clouds.

They shall travel like a whirlwind. The earth shall stagger like a drunken man. Twothirds of all the people of the earth will perish but the righteous shall be saved.

Are we soon to see some of the Bible's greatest prophecies fulfilled?

These thoughts filled my mind as if planted there by some supreme force over which I had no control.

At this point I heard the horn blowing on Jim's Dodge and looked up in time to see him pull over to the right side of the road. He had a very flat front tire. I pulled over and parked about four car lengths ahead of Jim's car. Harold also pulled off to the side. As Jim's spare was also flat and his wheels were the same size as mine, I proceeded to remove the spare wheel from the rear of my car, and we soon had Jim's car ready for action again.

However, as we happened to be near a small roadside cafe just outside the town of Riverside, Stella suggested that we all go in and have a cup of coffee.

While we were engaged in sipping our Java, a young lady who apparently was a good friend of one of the waitresses came in and sat diagonally across from me at the counter. She was very excited and began to tell of how she and a boy friend, while parking in the moonlight a few nights previously, had watched three flying saucers caper across the sky at close range She said that several times they appeared to hover directly in front of the moon as if to better display themselves to onlookers..

After they had been watching them for about fifteen minutes the three shiny craft moved slowly away from the moon and continued to travel slowly north. Then they suddenly shifted course, heading east toward the desert. and streaked out of sight so fast that they vanished from view completely in about five seconds.

Of course there was the usual display of skepticism from those present and someone remarked in a low Voice that there must have been some good stuff in that bottle. One couple displayed their ill-breeding getting up and leaving with the remark:

"Let s get out of this nuthouse!"

I then thought to myself: I would sure love to see one of those Saucers, but if I ever do I'll keep still about it.

Two Nights to Remember

The young lady went on to describe in detail the mysterious spacecraft, and how they seemed to glow with a fluorescent halo which seemed to change color as they increased or decreased speed.

At this point the laughter became so hilarious that the poor girl left feeling very bad indeed that should have been the object of such fun making. I could not help feeling very sorry for her as she walked dejectedly down the sidewalk. I thought to myself: we will always have our doubting Thomases. People are that way.

Someone had dropped a nickel in the juke box and the volume was turned up so loud that I had to ask the waitress three times how much our bill was. Considering this, plus the fact that the poor young lady who had had the rare privilege to witness these craft from outer space had practically been laughed out of the place, I felt glad to once more step foot on God's good earth.

I thought of how Christ had been ridiculed and stoned by those who would not listen to the truths he was trying to impart, and I thought also how wicked was this earth on which we lived - of our feverish efforts to engineer and develop weapons of such a destructive nature that they might soon rupture the very crust of our globe, vaporizing millions of innocent women, children and men, who have no say whatsoever in the matter. Perhaps this is the reason the very Angels of God are standing by.

By this time we were all comfortably seated in our

respective cars and once more were ready to resume our journey. bite drove east through the very beautiful little town of Sunnymead, then on to Beaumont, and then to Banning. We were now in the desert. Once more we stopped for coffee, this time at the Greyhound Bus Terminal. We decided the coffee would be good here.

After chatting for about fifteen minutes, and after listening patiently to the advice of an old timer who had noticed our camping equipment to watch out at this time of year for sidewinders, we once more headed down the road toward Desert Hot Springs, this time with Jim in the lead.

Soon Harold gave us a couple of blasts on his wolf whistle and roared past, leasing us in the rear. We knew however that this was a playful gesture on the part of both Harold and Jim, and they would soon fall back so I could lead the way to our final destination.

We were now heading toward Palm Springs. As we drove past the little town of Whitevater, beautiful Mt. San Gorgonio rose majestically to our left, and I wondered if there were not gold in 'them thar hills.

We were now at the turn off in the highway. We bore left at the World and headed now toward Indio. At this point Jim and Harold, who were no longer sure of the route, pulled their cars to the side of the road and signaled for me to again take the lead. This I did, and soon we turned left on the 29 Palms Highway. As we continued up the steep grade that leads up to the high desert, the sun was sinking low in the western sky and as it sank slowly down behind Mt. San

Two Nights to Remember

Gorgonio, it was truly a wonderful sight to behold. I realized none as I had many times before, why California was called the Golden State.

A halo of gold extended far above the mountain tops and blended into the beautiful blue or the desert sky, while billowy white clouds drifted leisurely above. The magnificent scene continuously changed with every turn of the road, and I wished many times that I had not forgotten to take along my 35mm camera. But it had been left behind in our rush to get started.

We had planned for days to tale this trip to the desert and had carefully made a list of the things to take along. Now here we were, a hundred miles from home and no camera. Of course Stella had her old Brownie box camera, but it was loaded with black and white film and practically useless for photographing a beautiful rare sunset. While at home, lying at the foot of our bcd, was my expensive 35mm camera, all loaded with color film.

As I drove along thus reminiscing. I had failed to notice that both Bettyann and Bobby, who had been unusually quiet since leaving Banning, were now asleep in the back seat. Stella had also started to nod at my side and I now began to realize that I had been the only one in our car who had marveled at the beautiful golden sunset. I wondered if those in the other cars had been a witness to this good display of nature.

I now turned off the 29 Palms Highwav and drove toward Descrt Hot Springs. As we made the town, Harold sounded his horn and looking into my rear view mirror, I noticed him signal for me to stop. Pulling up the emergency brake, I ran back to see why he had stopped.

By this time Stella, Bettyann and Bobby were all fully awakened by the lurching of the car.

As I approached Harold's car, he explained that Jim and Terry had fallen behind on the last hill and we should wait for them to catch us, as Jim would not be aware of the turn we had just taken. As we stood talking Jim's car came slowly over the crest of the hill. Stepping out of his car Harold waved to Jim to follow us.

It was now beginning to grow quite dark. As we all lighted up our cigarettes and prepared once more to move on, Jim remarked that we would have a hard time trying to select a good camp site in the darkness. To this we all agreed and I suggested that we start looking at once.

We drove south on a paved road, not knowing where it would take us. I don't know how many miles it was - at least five or six - when I spotted a dirt road leading from my left. I started to pass it by when suddenly the strangest thing happened. I I seemed that some uncontrollable unseen force started to turn the steering wheel. I immediately thought that something had gone wrong with the steering mechanism. And then a voice yes, a definite voice - whispered in my ear.

It said, "Turn here, drive three miles and stop." I looked at Stella, who had been startled by the quick turn to the left, and asked: "Did you speak to me just then? Did you whisper in my ear?"

She looked at me as if I had suddenly gone mad.

"Why of course not," she replied. "Why should I whisper in your ear? And why on earth did you decide to turn so suddenly?"

I was now thoroughly confused, and thought that I must surely be cracking up, so I meekly remarked, "Guess I must be hearing things."

At this point Bettyann called from the back seat, "Daddy, when are we going to stop. I'm getting hungry. And how are we going to set up the tent in the dark?"

"Yes," joined in Bob, "I'm starved. I could eat a jack rabbit."

Just then, ironically enough, a huge jack rabbit ran in front of the headlights of our car, pausing just long enough to sit up a moment, as if dazed by the bright lights, and then scurried off across the desert into the darkness.

Needless to say, this incident brought laughs from all, and Bettyann giggled:

"There's your supper, Bob."

The road at this point was very rough. The sand was deep in places and the car slowed down until I had to change to second gear.

Two Nights to Remember

Huge Joshua trees loomed up in the car's headlights like weird, grotesque monsters. A coyote scurried across the sand in the distant beam of the car's lights.

"In the name of heaven when are you going to stop?" cried Stella.

"Not until we drive three miles from the paved road where we turned off,' I replied, as I glanced at the speedometer. We have one mile to go yet."

"John three miles?" asked everyone in a chorus.

"Never mind. You would never understand," I replied.

"You are certainly in a fine frame of mind, I must say" retorted Stclla. "You must be getting tired of driving. You had better stop now."

"I'll stop at the end of the three miles," I snapped.

I could have bitten my tongue for the way I shouted at my wife. But I could not understand the strange feeling that possessed me since I had heard the strange voice in my car. It had seemed as if I had suddenly been bathed from head to foot in lukewarm water and the voice had actually seemed to come from inside my head, neither in my right nor in my left ear, but from somewhere inside my brain. It is difficult to describe.

I could hear the racing of Harold's motor in back of us as he shifted gears to pull through the sand.

Two Nights to Remember

At this point the dirt road seemed to end, and now we were going slightly down hill. The sugar-like sand now seemed to be changing to a hard decomposed granite formation, and we now had no more difficulty in proceeding.

"We are nearly there," I remarked as I glanced once more at the speedometer. "Two-tenths of a mile more and we'll make camp."

"It's about time," replied Stella.

We now seemed to be on the bottom of an ancient dry lake-bed. The surface of the desert was hard and smooth. I pulled to a stop and stepped out of the car. It seemed good to get out and stretch and breathe the cool clean desert air. Millions of stars shone overhead and some of them seemed close enough to pluck. In the dim starlight we could make out our surroundings. We seemed to be hemmed in from all sides by mountains, and the lake-bed on which we were was level and devoid of cactus or Joshua trees. In fact, it almost looked like a small air-strip or landing field

"Gosh, Carl, I thought you were never going to stop!" exclaimed Jim. "Terry is starving. Let's get some hot coffee going."

I dragged the camp stove from the rear of my car and set it up on the stand provided for it. The girls all turned to and started to prepare hot soup and coffee for all. We soon had two Coleman Gas Lanterns burning and while Harold, Jim and myself were setting up the tent, Bettyann and Bobby had built a fire to toast marshmallows, with wood that Jim had brought along for the occasion.

Soon he four army cots were ready in the tent. It was getting late and Bobby and Betty were tired and ready for bed. Stella tucked them in and tied the tent flap. The rest of us sat around the campfire eating toasted marshmallows, spinning yarns and puffing an occasional cigarette. It was a very beautiful and warm night on the desert. The usual evening chill did not prevail. It was such a wonderful night that no one wanted to turn in. The desert air was refreshing and invigorating.

We talked of many things but most of all about other people. People much like us perhaps, on far distant worlds, and we wondered as we gazed into thc skies above if we would be lucky enough to see a flying saucer. Oh, how we wished one would land and contact us. But as the evening wore on, and it got well past midnight. we finallly decided to turn in. Stella and I had the two cots on one side of the tent, while Bettyann and Bobby occupied the others.

We crept quietly to our beds, not wishing to awaken the children.

Harold and Eleanor bedded down in their car, as did also Tim and Terry. Harold's Buick was parked about thirty feet from our tent. Jim's Dodge was about fifty feet away.

As I lay awake in my tent, I wondered about the strange voice and I also wondered if we had actually been directed to this remote and desolate spot for some specific purpose. Could the strange voice and the strange feeling that had penetrated my body from head to toe, be a message in telepathy? And what about the strange feeling that someone else had turned the car onto the dirt road that had led us to this lonely spot. I was much confused to say the least, and I pondered over these very strange events until, at last, sleep overtook me.

How long I slept I do not know. Suddenly I was wide awake and sitting upright on the cot. Stella and Bettyann were also sitting up, but Bobby was still sleeping soundly.

As the three of us sat there wondering what had awakened us a miracle happened. The tent slowly began to disappear until it became absolutely invisible and, looking out across the desert, I beheld a very privileged sight. There, apparently hovering a few inches off the ground, was a large shinning disc. There was no doubt in my mind that this was a flying saucer.

The diameter of this craft from outer space was about sixty feet, and it was about twenty-five or thirty feet in height. Five windows, or portholes, were visible from where we were. The unearthly vehicle glowed all over with a dull fluorescent light. A sort of halo seemed to surround the entire craft. I could not tell whether or not it had any sort of landing gear. I did not see any. It appeared to hover in space about eighteen to twenty inches off the ground.

I tried to move toward this object. I wanted to go over and touch it, but I found that I could not move an

inch. I was completely paralyzed. Stella and Bettyann later said they had the very same experience. The mysterious force that had changed the frequency vibrations which had caused our tent to become invisible also held us prisoners by paralyzing us completely. I did however manage to roll my eyes enough to glance at my wrist watch. The luminous dial read three o'clock (A.M.).

Two Nights to Remember

We did not know at the time just how long we remained in this paralyzed condition while we continued to watch and listen. We could now hear voices mumbling in a low tone, but could not tell, however, if the conversation was in English, as the sounds were very faint.

We do not know whether or not any people alighted from this craft. We did not see any. But we did hear voices.

After what seemed like hours we began to hear a slight humming sound like a generator running.

A low droning, pulsating hum. The dim glow surrounding the Saucer slowly took on an orange cast, then a bright red color. It glowed like a huge ball of red fire. Then it started to rise straight up, very slowly at first, then faster and faster as it got higher and higher. The red light changed to a brilliant bluish white. Then slowly the tent began to reappear and once more we were aware of its presence. As the tent became a reality we were once more free to move about. We now realized that we had been paralyzed for our own good. It was not meant for us to go near or touch this wonderful craft from another world.

We sprang to our feet and looked out through the tent flap. The brilliant blue white light was streaking across the sky and soon disappeared over the horizon near Mt. San Gorgonio.

Bettyann's first words were, "Daddy, where did the tent go? And why couldn't I move?"

Two Nights to Remember

Harold and Eleanor had had the same identical experience. They had also been paralyzed and the car in which they were had become invisible. But strangely enough Jim and Terry, being farther away in their car, had not even been awakened, and were dumbfounded when told of the Saucer's visit.

The next morning I took a picture, with Stella's camera, of the spot where the strange ship from outer space had hovered. When the film was developed this picture was the only one on the entire roll that showed very peculiar lines emanating from the ground, as heat waves appear on a hot day. These particular waves, however, were no doubt some kind of radiation from the spacecraft which had been absorbed by the ground - perhaps the same invisible force that had caused the tent and the car to disappear and had paralyzed us.

However we suffered no ill effects at any time from our contact with this force. The next morning the clock in my car, which had been at some distance from the Saucer, was fifteen minutes faster than my wrist watch, indicating that my watch had stopped at three a.m. for a period of fifteen minutes. The paralyzing rays had evidently stopped it. Since my watch is self-winding it must have started again when the craft took off. This indicates to me that the Saucer remained on the ground for about fifteen minutes. I have not known this watch to ever stop before or since this incident.

This is one night I shall always remember, for as we watched the fiery red vehicle ascending into the skies, who is to say it was not the same as Elijah's fiery chariot?

There was very little sleep for any of us during the remainder of that night and as the sun rose over the mountains to the east we were up to greet it. After eating a hearty breakfast of bacon, eggs, and coffee we all felt much better. The things we had witnessed but a few hours before now seemed a long way off. I now knew that spacecraft and flying saucers were not only a reality, but I felt more sure than ever before that the occupants of these crafts were none other than the Angels of the Lord. Certainly no earthly being could ever perform such miracles.

The trip home was uneventful. we were all refreshed from our visit in the sunshine and fresh air of the high desert.

Two Nights to Remember

As Jim and Terry had not been fortunate enough to see the magnificent craft from Outer space they were anxious to pay another visit to the desert at the earliest opportunity. But I felt deep inside me that I had now established mental contact with these space people and that I would know when to again seek out a remote spot for contacting their craft at some future date.

I felt that my faith in their existence had been proven by their visit. and that now I knew of their presence, they would again come at their convenience and not just because I desired them. But that when they did come I would know in advance. and that certain circumstances would lead me to a rendezvous. I had a very definite feeling that they would contact me again but I knew not when.

Little did I know that I was destined to again see this beautiful ship from another world, just eighteen months in the future.

The days, the weeks, and the months passed slowly by. Being an employee of the Navy Yard at Long Beach, I am allotted one month vacation time with pay each year.

Vacation time had rolled around. It was August of 1955, and we looked forward to a wonderful two weeks at Yosemite National Park.

Upon arriving in the Park, we chose a desirable camp site and again pitched our umbrella tent. Bobby and Bettyann, of course, did their share to make sure we would have a comfortable two weeks' stay.

We had a wonderful time hiking up the trails to the many beautiful waterfalls, fishing for the wary trout that we could not catch, swimming in Mirror Lake and the Merced River, which flows through the valley, driving up to spectacular Glacier Point - from which one can see, for many miles in all directions, the rugged snow-capped peaks of the mighty Sierra Nevada Mountains.

We visited the fish hatcheries at famous Happy Isles, explored the Indian Caves, gazing in reverence at the awe-inspiring spectacles of El Capitan and the mighty Half Dome, an entire mountain of solid granite which has been cut completely in two by the tremendous weight and pressure of the gigantic sheet of glacier ice of some distant period far beyond the memory of man.

We playfully sounded our auto horn while driving through the famous Wawona Tunnel, and strolled among the oldest and largest of all known living things, the mighty Sequoia trees.We watched the deer begging food from the campers and the huge bears that tip over the garbage cans—a noise which woke us from our sleep so many nights.

One night after we had watched the famous fire falls three thousand feet above Camp Curry, Stella and I were walking back to our camp. Bobby and Bettann had remained back at the tent of an adjoining camper, as they had been invited to a wiener roast. As we strolled silently across a small meadow looking up at the myriad stars in the heavens above. we suddenly saw two of the familiar blue-white lights approaching from the east.

As they passed directly overhead the lights changed to a bright orange hue as if they knew we were watching, then turned at a forty-five degree angle and continued on in a northerly direction the lights again changing to the familiar blue-white color. They then disappeared over the horizon and we're gone in a flash. As the lights turned to orange. I again had that strange but now familiar feeling come over me from head to toe a feeling as if warm water was being poured over me and I knew that once more I had received a message from space, even as others had received inspirations and messages over two thousand years ago.

I often wonder how long these people from other planets live. The Bible tells us that the ways of sin is death. It would therefore indicate where there is no sin there would be no death. Perhaps other worlds have no sin. This is certainly something to think about.

Our two week stay at Yosemite passed very pleasantly and all too quickly. Bettyann and Bobby were, of course, quite excited when we told them of having seen two more Saucers, and during the long trip home they watched the skies almost continuously in hope of catching a glimpse of a silvery shining ship from outer space.

When I told of our sightings after returning to work I, of course, received the same type of skepticism as before by those unfortunate co-workers who had chosen to refrain from any belief in space visitors. There were, however, a few of my associates whose soul evolution had progressed sufficiently to accept not only the possibility but also the extreme probability that flying saucers were an actual reality. And there were also a few who professed to have seen them high in the skies, especially during the long summer evenings.

About two weeks after my return to work I chanced to be working near the number one Dry Dock. I was busily engaged in making an electrical installation when suddenly I felt that familiar feeling of warmth flow over my entire body as if I had been dunked in warm water. Instantly I gazed skyward. It was two o'clock and a beautiful summer afternoon. The azure blue sky was nearly cloudless. Only a few small fleecy white clouds drifted slowly overhead. At first I saw nothing but a few sea gulls winging their way high above me.

Had I been mistaken? Had I only imagined I had received again that now familiar message? I was about to resume my duties when suddenly there it was, a beautiful huge silvery disc high above and almost directly over the spot upon which I stood. It was of tremendous size and hovered perfectly motionless. I shouted excitedly and pointed skyward. Two of my fellow workers came running to investigate the excitement. One of them exclaimed, "My God, what is that?"

As if in answer the huge disc seemed to turn on its side and roll across the sky like a gigantic wheel. It stopped abruptly and shot straight up out of sight. As we watched, it again appeared and slowly circled, then started to descend. As we continued to watch, it made several ninety degree turns, as if its operator were trying to exhibit his skill.

Suddenly we heard the familiar swish and roar of a jet plane. As we watched a jet fighter appeared, streaking swiftly toward this huge shinning Saucer which was now hovering. On rushed the jet until it seemed that it would surely crash into this monster from another world. Then quick as a flash the huge silver disc shot to one side and the jet missed it by a very wide margin. The speed of the jet took it 'way off over the city before its pilot could finally circle and start back.

The first performance was repeated. This time the jet seemed to fly even faster than before, but to no avail. The Saucer neatly avoided the plane. Making another wide circle, the jet returned. This time its tactics were different. It went into a steep dive then started to climb like a streak of lightning straight up beneath the space visitor, and a third time it was a complete miss, as the Saucer darted to the side and then shot straight up and disappeared.

After circling the area several times. and its pilot apparently feeling very dejected at the outcome of this cat and mouse game, the jet left and did not return. Needless to say, my two co-workers, having seen for themselves, Nowhere no longer doubting Thomases and even offered me their apologies.

This entire episode must have lasted at least ten minutes and certainly must have been seen by others. But as usual, not a word appeared in the press.

Two Nights to Remember

Another evening shortly after, as thousands of workers starting home from work in broad daylight, a large ball of fire came streaking across the sky. Many thought it was a plane on fire, but suddenly it stopped, and remained suspended and motionless. As hundreds watched, it suddenly shot straight up out of sight and dissapeared. Of course, this was no plane on fire. And it was seen by many. Yet this incident likewise did not appear in the press.

The months rolled by and I continued to search the skies. On many occasions during the twilight hours I have seen those familiar discs high overhead and have called my family as well as several neighbors to witness their presence.

Finally the thing I had so long waited for came to pass. I began to get an uncontrolable urge to once more seek peace and solitude in the desert. As the days passed the urge grew stronger and stronger until I finally announced to my wife and to Jim that we were once more to spend the weekend in the most desolate spot we could find. This time we decided to sleep under the stars without the tent. As we only had three sleeping bags, and as Terry was not well enough to rough it, Stella, |Jim, and myself decided to go.

My older daughter Janet, who is married, was spending the weekend with us, as her husband, Denis, had had other commitments with Uncle Sam's Marine Corps. Janet would stay with Bobby and Bettyann. So it w as about eighteen months after our first contact near Desert Hot Springs that we started once more for the wide open spaces. It was the first

Two Nights to Remember

weekend of October, 1955.

This time we decided to take only my car since only the three of us were going. We left my home in Lakewood shortly after noon and proceeded to drive once more to Desert Hot Springs. Our trip was uneventful and we stopped only for gas and cigarettes. As we came to the turn-off for Desert Hot Springs I proceeded to turn to the right Then it happened again. This time I heard no voice, but felt a very definite tug at the wheel. I could not move it to the right and before I realized what had taken place, had passed the road leading to Desert Hot Springs.

As if to reassure me that I should continue on, that familiar warm tingling sensation surged through my body. I now had not the slighest idea of where we were going. Jim had reminded me of my failure to make the turn. I could only reply that there had been a change in plans.

We were now heading toward Twenty-Nine Palms, and I had not the slighest idea of our destination. We passed through the little desert town of Morongo Valley. Here we stopped to fill up the gas tank. I knew not where we were going, but I wanted to be sure of enough gas to get there.

Next we passed through the town of Yucca Valley. We proceeded down a long grade and now saw a road to the left. The highway sign indicated this road led to the desert town of Victorville. That warm feeling now returned. I did not wait for further instructions but immediately turned left.

Two Nights to Remember

Soon we were climbing up a very steep hill, and after about ten miles or so the pavement came to an abrupt ending. From here on it appeared to be a dirt road. We had to greatly decrease our slated, as the road was very rough and extremely dusty.

I saw many minor roads leading off to both sides. Stella and Jim continued to question me as to where we were going. I could not tell them; I did not know.

I drove for what seemed like miles, then once again I heard the voice. It said, "Turn left."

This tirme I did not feel the warm glow permeate my being, but the voice was unmistakably real. I watched closely for a left turn. But none appeared. I had almost convinced myself that I must have been mistaken when, as we rounded a bend in the road, I saw a faint trail leading to the left. Was this it? It was certainly very little used; however, I played a hunch and turned. As I did so, that familiar warmth tingled through me and I now knew I had received the answer.

I continued on into the desert. We were now heading straight toward Mt. San Gorgonio. Huge Joshua trees appeared on all sides. Jack rabbits scampered everywhere and several large lizards clung to granite boulders on both sides, basking in the afternoon sun. The trail became almost impassable. Upon rounding a sharp bend we once more came upon what appeared to be a small dry lake-bed. We could go no farther as we were surrounded by huge boulders, but the lake-bed clearing was perhaps five hundred yards across.

Two Nights to Remember

As I sat there wondering if this were my appointed destination, the motor of my car stopped. Looking toward the instrument panel I discovered to my amazement that the ignition key had been turned off. Both Stella and Jim. who were beside me, denied having any knowledge of this mysterious occurrence. This we immediately took to be our answer. Yes, this was the spot where we would camp.

The sun was now sinking low, and we were hungry from our trip and the refreshing desert air. We knew that as soon as it became sundown it would no doubt become chilly, as it was now October and the elevation was better than three thousand feet. We gathered up pieces of dead Joshua limbs, sagebrush and mesquite to supplement the meager supply of firewood that we had thrown into the back of my car. While dragging out the wood two emergency red flares fell to the ground. I had carried these in the rear compartment for many months, since one never knows when they may be needed. Jim stuck them into the sand and remarked, "Let's light them tonight and have some fireworks. They will look pretty after dark."

After warming up a couple of cans of beans on the gasoline stove we set up cur portable table and dug in with gusto. Using paper plates, we soon disposed of all dirty dishes. We then spread our sleeping bags out on the sand and started a campfire.

As the evening wore on, the chill air we had expected drifted down from the mountains. and we were glad that we had all brought our leather jackets. We sat close to the fire. chatting. drinking an occasional cup of coffee and puffing cigarettes. Stella turned on the car radio and left the door open. Reception was vary poor in this spot. The program kept fading and much static persisted. Stella finally got up and turned it off. As she turned back toward Tim and I her teeth chattered slightly from the cool night breeze and she remarked. "I'm going to wear everything but my shoes when I crawl into that sleeping bag."

"That's a good idea," agreed Jim.

The fire was now getting low and we decided to slip into our sacks. We lay there in the dim glow of the waning fire and gazed at the cold, clear, cloudless skies overhead. As we watched the Big Dipper in the northern sky, I kept a sharp lookout for our space friends. This time I knew without a doubt that they would appear. Not because I wanted it that way, but because of the uncontrolable urge that had possessed me to return to the desert. And I had not the slightest doubt they would soon show up.

Soon it would be midnight. The sleeping bags were unbelievably warm. We could hear the occasional howl of a lone coyote in the distance.

Suddenly from over the top of Mt. San Gorgonio a brilliant bluish-white light came streaking straight toward us. It traveled far too fast to be a plane, even a jet. It made no sound of any kind. It was now circling slowly overhead. The light turned to a dull green, then white, but this time more of a faint glow like a halo. Slowly, very slowly, it started to descend.

Two Nights to Remember

We were now all on our feet, watching and waiting. The moon shone on this huge craft, and we could look straight up from beneath. It looked like a plate slowly falling. We all waited in joyous anticipation of the landing that we felt sure they would make. Down came the great shinning Saucer. It seemed that it might land in the very spot on which we stood. We were all prepared to move aside.

The great craft was now scarcely two hundred feet overhead. We could now make out what appeared to be three large round ball-like objects, equally spaced in thirds near the outer rim of the ship, from which the fluorescent glowing light appeared to emanate. The great craft seemed to bounce up and down slightly, as if the earth's gravity were gradually being canceled out. We could hear the pulsating hum. Each time the craft bounced the hum would increase, then decrease. It was now scarcely one hundred feet off the ground. It's size was tremendous.

Suddenly, for a reason that she does not know to this day, Stella became panic-stricken. This was the very first time she had ever shown any fright. Running toward the car, she cried out in terror, "Oh, my God !"

The occupants of the great Saucer seemed to know instantly of her fright. While she sobbed like a child, the great Saucer shot swiftly up and hovered high above.

As Jim stirred up the fire I tried to comfort my wife, and finally succeeded in assuring her that these beings would do us no harm. She now had control of her emotions and came over by the fire. The Saucer still hovered above. Reaching down and grasping one of the flares which was still stuck in the sand, Jim lighted it. Holding it high in the air he continued to wave it about in a circular motion.

"Let's signal for them to come down and land," cried Jim.

The great shining ship began once more to settle lower and lower. Suddenly Jim threw the burning torch to the ground with a cry of pain. The burning chemicals had dripped down on his right thumb. causing a severe and extremely painful burn.

The Saucer checked its descent but continued to hover, while Jim rushed to my car and turned on the headlights to examine his injuries. Stella and I both saw the swollen and very badly burned thumb.

Two Nights to Remember

As Jim looked up at the great disc still hovering above he cried out, "Oh, God! Why did this have to happen?"

At that instant, the dull fluorescent glow around the rim of the huge craft started to brighten. It turned to a brilliant white and then disappeared. The great Saucer had gone, exactly as if a light had been switched off. We all stood there staring up, fascinated by what we had just seen. The wicked burn on Jim's thumb had been forgotten - even by Jim himself.

The great craft from another world was now gone and I broke the silence finally by suggesting that we put a bandage on Jim's thumb. His attention now focused hack on his injury, Jim dashed for the beam of th car's headlights.

"I can't believe it," he murmured. "It's a miracle.' Stella and I gathered round. Yes, another miracle had been performed by God's Angels. Only moments before we had looked at a very severely burned thumb, we had heard Jim cry out in pain we had seen the agony on his face. We were now looking at the same thumb. But not a trace of a burn existed. Yes, truly, a miracle had taken place once more before our very eyes.

If not representatives of the Almighty Creator who other can these people be? Who else could cause the tent to become invisible? Who else could create mass paralysis without ill after effects? Who else could have completely healed Jim's burned thumb - which was so completely healed that even the experiment of rubbing sand on it did not bother him.

Yes, this is the other night I shall always remember. I have never since had the urge to be drawn to the desert, although I am sure if and when I do have the good fortune to receive another mental communication I shall also see more of our space benefactors.

I would like to again remind the reader that the contents of this book are not fiction. that the incidents actually happened as described. But I know that there will always be disbelievers. I, myself. was such a strong disbeliever when I first heard about flying saucers and people from other worlds that this may be the reason they chose to reveal to me not only their existence, but the supreme power they can manifest.

We all feel very certain that the people of the second

craft contacted fully intended to land and make themselves known to us. Had it not been for my wife's fear, we may have even been taken aboard. Who knows? After summing up what has happened. I am now convinced more than ever before that life on this Earth planet is only a class room in eternity? that we reincarnate at death and are reborn on a higher plane. for the Bible states thou shalt be born again I believe that man has miserably flunked in this grade with his wickedness and destructive ways.

I believe the atom is for God to control and that man is overstepping his bounds. I believe that the spacecraft are standing by to assist us and show us the Light. I believe they will make certain that there is never an atomic war, for they will instill in the minds of all men the love and mercy of the Father, and one day soon - yes, sooner than we think - a new age will be upon us, an age of peace on earth and love toward all creatures and all fellow men. That is when the lamb shall lie down with the lion, and the child shall play with the asp. Yes, I believe we are now entering the long awaited millenium and that Christ has already returned in spirit to organize His Kingdom on Earth. His Angels are standing by, and one day soon, Christ himself will come down in all his glory.

In the meantime, I am very sure that the reader who has the eyes to see the Light, will agree that I have indeed *Two Nights to Remember*.

APPENDIX

Because of the very strange and unusual nature of the events described in this book we append the affidavits of the several people who were present with Mr. Anderson and witnessed the amazing series of happenings. This would not be necessary for people who know the Andersons, nor for those who have had experiences connected with flying saucers and their occupants which were too fantastic to relate, but for the average reader to whom such occurrences are so foreign to his own experience as to seem incredible it will serve to reassure such a one of the reality of the remarkable series of events which took place during Two Nights to Remember.

These affidavits were not made at the time but several months afterward at the suggestion of the publisher. Even though the first excitement had somewhat abated the experiences were still so vivid to all that they were without exception willing to place themselves on record in corroboration of the statements made by Mr. Anderson regarding what happened during two memorable nights under the stars on the great Mojave desert.

Affidavits

Two Nights to Remember

Stella Anderson

Date *May-17-1956*

To whom it may concern;

This is to certify that I, Stella Dee Anderson, did on
two separate and individual occasions, witness Spacecraft
known as flying Saucers, in the Calif. desert. One near
Desert Center, the other, south of Victorville Calif.
on the dates of April 4, 1954 and on October 2, 1955
And that on one occasion, a beam or ray of some kind which I
believe is unknown to earthly science, caused my husband,
my daughter, and myself to be completely paralyzed until
the Saucer left. During this period, about fifteen minutes,
a tent in which we were, became invisible to the eye. And
that on the other occasion, I witnessed the miraculous
healing of a severe burn on the right thumb of my brother
James E. Stewart, which had just been caused by a burning
flare he was using to signal the Saucer with. This healing
was accomplished, I believe, by the same ray or beam from
this huge Saucer which was hovering above us. The statements
herein contained, are true to the best of my knowledge and
belief.

Stella D. Anderson

Signed this...17th... day of...May... 19.56.
Witness...*Herbert P. Smith*...

HERBERT P. SMITH, Notary Public
in and for the County of Los Angeles, State of California
My Commission Expires July 27, 1958
9445 E. Flower, Bellflower, Calif.

Two Nights to Remember

Bettyann Anderson

Date May 17-1956

To whom it may concern;

This is to certify that I, Bettyann Louise Anderson, did
see a Craft known as a flying Saucer, hover near a tent in
which I was sleeping, with my mother and father on the night
of April 4, 1954 near Desert Center, Calif. and that some
strange force held the three of us captive by means of
paralyzing us to the extent that we were unable to move, or
to talk, until the Saucer left. A period of about fifteen
minutes. This same force, also rendered our tent to become
invisible to the eye. I believe this was caused by a ray or
a beam of which our earthly science knows nothing.

The foregoing statements are true to the best of my knowledge
and belief. *Bettyann L Anderson*

Signed this....12...... day of May...... 195.7..

Witness.....*Herbert P. Smith*................

HERBERT P. SMITH, Notary Public
in and for the County of Los Angeles, State of California
My Commission Expires July 27, 1955
9445 E Flower. Bellflower, Calif.

48

Two Nights to Remember

Harold Stewart

Date. *May 14, 1956*

To whom it may concern;

This is to certify that I, Harold L. Stewart, did on the
4th. day of April in the year 1954 witness what I consider
to be a flying Saucer hover close to the ground in the
vicinity of Desert Center, in the Calif. desert for a period
of several minutes, during which time I was held in a state
of paralysis which I consider to have been caused by some type
of beam from this object. I also witnessed the automobile
in which I had been sleeping, suddenly become invisible.
The above is true, to the best of my knowledge and belief.

Signed this... *14*..... day of. *May*.... 19.*56*.
Witness.... *Eleanor C. Stewart*....

Harold L. Stewart

Robert Hill Shore

My Commission Expires Feb. 4, 1959

Two Nights to Remember

Eleanor Stewart

Date May 14, 1956

To whom it may concern;

This is to certify that I Eleanor Stewart, did on the
4th. day of April in the year 1954 witness a large
shining object hovering close to the ground in the
Calif. Desert in a remote spot near Desert Center.
I also had the experience of being totaly and completely paralyzed, which I believe was caused by an
invisible ray of some kind from this object, which I
consider to have been a flying Saucer, until this object
went straight into the air and disappeared.
This is true, to the best of my knowledge and belief.

Signed this May 14., day of May. 19.5.6.
Witness.....................................

Eleanor A. Stewart

Robert Hill Mayer

My Commission Expires Feb. 4, 1959

Two Nights to Remember

James Stewart

Date. *May. 14, 1956*

To whom it may concern;

This is to certify that I James E. Stewart, did on or about
the 2nd. day of October in the year 1955 witness a huge
object hovering above me on the Calif. desert in a remote
spot south of Victorville. I also had the uncanny experience
of having a severe burn which I had suffered from a burning
flare, miraculously healed, as this object changed color.
I believe this was accomplished by some kind of beam or ray
unknown to our science here on earth.

The statements contained herein are true to the best of my
knowledge and belief. *James E. Stewart*

Signed this.. *14 th* .... day of.. *May*... 19.*56*..

Witness.*of Signature*........ *Don Jones*

DON JONES. Notary Public
In and for the County of Los A . . . . State of Califat
My Commission Expires Apr. 16, 1960
2545 Fashion Ave., Long Beach, Calif.

www.ingramcontent.com/pod-product-compliance
Lightning Source LLC
Chambersburg PA
CBHW071113090426
42737CB00013B/2585